Cambridge English Readers

Level 2

Series editor: Philip

Apollo's Gold

Antoinette Moses

CAMBRIDGE

CAMBRIDGE UNIVERSITY PRESS
Cambridge, New York, Melbourne, Madrid, Cape Town, Singapore, São Paulo

Cambridge University Press
The Edinburgh Building, Cambridge CB2 2RU, UK

www.cambridge.org
Information on this title: www.cambridge.org/9780521775533

First published 1999
8th printing 2005

Printed in Italy by Legoprint S.p.A.

A catalogue record for this publication is available from the British Library

ISBN-13 978-0-521-77553-3 paperback
ISBN-10 0-521-77553-1 paperback
ISBN-13 978-0-521-77547-2 cassette
ISBN-10 0-521-77547-7 cassette

Illustrations by Mike Dodd

Contents

People in the story

Liz: an English archaeologist, twenty-seven years old, works in Athens.

Stavros: Liz's boss, a professor of archaeology.

Eleni: she has a restaurant in Poulati on Sifnos.

Yiannis: Eleni's brother, a fisherman.

Nikos: a policeman on Sifnos.

Takis, **Mike and Mr John**: three men on a yacht.

GREECE

Athens

SIFNOS

Milos

Aghios
Sostis

Kamares

Poulati*

Apollonia

400m 600m 200m

200m

SIFNOS

N

0   1   2   3 kms

*Poulati is not a real town

Chapter 1 *Get well!*

It began with a visit to the doctor. 'You need a holiday,' the doctor told me. 'You need a rest.'

'I can't take a holiday,' I answered. 'I'm too busy.'

'No, Liz,' said the doctor. 'You don't understand. If you don't take a holiday, you're going to get very, very ill.'

'I'm just tired,' I said. 'I feel tired.'

'No,' he said. 'It's more than that. Are you doing too much? You teach, don't you?'

'Well, yes,' I said. 'I'm teaching and studying archaeology at the university.'

'What else are you doing?' he asked me.

'I'm learning to speak Greek,' I replied. 'And I'm writing a book.'

'I see,' he said. 'You're learning to speak Greek, you're writing a book and you're working at the university. Don't you think that's too much? How many hours do you sleep at night?'

'Four or five hours most nights,' I told him.

'It's not enough,' he said. 'You need to slow down. Is your husband here in Greece with you?' the doctor asked.

'No,' I told the doctor. 'I was married but my husband left me. Last year.'

'I understand,' said the doctor.

'No,' I thought, 'you don't really understand. Because you don't know that my husband left me and went to live with one of his students. Because you don't know that I am still very angry. I am both angry and sad. You don't understand because you don't know that I had to leave London to be away from my husband who is still working at London University.'

Only a year ago everything was wonderful. I had a good job in London. I had a wonderful husband. I loved him and he loved me. Or I thought he loved me. But then I found out that he was actually in love with someone else. My wonderful world wasn't real.

But that was a year ago. Now I lived in Greece and had a job I enjoyed. And I had a wonderful, kind boss, Stavros. Stavros looks like a big animal and has a black beard. But he's a very good archaeologist. Sometimes I think that he can feel what is under the earth, even before he begins to look for it. And he's very kind. I love working for him.

After I left the doctor's I went to see Stavros at the university.

Stavros is very big man, but his office is so untidy that sometimes it's hard to find him. As usual there were pots and bits of pots all over his desk. Stavros knows almost everything about Greek pots. Every day I spend with him, I learn something. When I walked into his office, he was looking through a magnifying glass.

'Oh!' I said. 'You've got that pot again. That's great.'

Stavros put down the magnifying glass. 'Yes,' he replied. 'The police gave the pot to me this morning. Two men were trying to take it out of the country. The police caught them at the airport.'

'That's wonderful,' I said. 'It's a lovely pot. It belongs here in Greece. In a museum.'

One of the biggest problems for all archaeologists is

stealing. As an archaeologist you want to find things because you want to learn about them. You want to learn about the people who lived in a place. You want to learn about the things they made. You can spend all your life looking at these pots and still learn new things. Pots tell you how people cooked and how they lived and what they did. But the people who steal just want to take the pots and make money. And usually they want to take them out of Greece.

Stealing is a problem for archaeologists in every country, but in Greece it's different. The problem is the sea. If you look at the things in the Greek museums, you will find that many of them were once under the sea. And there are still many wonderful things under the sea. So if you are rich and have a yacht, it's not difficult. You can dive and swim under the sea and if you find something, no-one knows. Archaeologists try to stop the divers. The police try to stop the divers. But it's not easy. The sea is very big and very empty.

I looked at the pot on Stavros's desk. It was two thousand years old.

Stavros was watching me. 'How are you, Liz?' he asked. 'You don't look well.'

'The doctor says that I need a holiday,' I told Stavros. 'But what shall I do?' I asked him. 'What about my students? What about my book? I can't just go away.'

'Yes, you can,' said Stavros. 'If the doctor says you need a holiday, then you must take a holiday. You must go. You're ill. Everyone can see that. You look terrible!'

'Thank you,' I said.

Stavros laughed. 'You know what I mean. Of course you don't really look terrible. You're always beautiful. But you do look ill.'

I don't think that I'm beautiful, but I know that I can look quite pretty. I'm tall with long legs and long brown hair. In the sun my hair begins to go blonde and that always makes me feel better. Some people say that I look a bit like the film star Julia Roberts. Perhaps I'm a little bit like her. But only on a good day. I don't look like a film star when I'm tired. I just look ill.

'Do you want to go back to London?' Stavros asked. He knows all about my husband, but he never talks about it. I often spend my weekends with Stavros and his family. He has three young children and we have lots of fun together.

'No,' I said. 'I want to stay here. Perhaps I could stay at home for a few days and just do a little writing.'

'No,' answered Stavros. 'The doctor was right. You need to go away. Go to an island. The islands are so beautiful in April. Lots of flowers and no tourists. You can stay in my house on Sifnos,' Stavros said.

'But I couldn't . . .' I began.

'Of course you could,' Stavros said. 'My family and I go there every summer, but it's empty now. It's very small, but it's clean and it has a bathroom and a kitchen.'

'Are you sure?' I asked him.

'Of course,' said Stavros. 'And you'll love Sifnos. My house is in a village called Poulati. It's a fishing village. It's beautiful.'

'Are you really sure?' I asked again.

'Yes,' he said. 'Of course I'm sure.'

'OK then,' I agreed. 'I'll go to Poulati. Thank you, Stavros. Thank you very much.'

'Fine,' Stavros said. 'My good friends Eleni and Yiannis live there. They're very friendly. I'll ring Eleni now. She has the key and lives next door. She owns the restaurant in Poulati, the *taverna*. Her brother Yiannis is a fisherman. I'll tell them that you are coming. Poulati is very quiet,' he said. 'It's a very special place. There's nothing to do there but rest and get well.'

Chapter 2   *Gold*

The boat for Sifnos left very early in the morning. Because it was April there were not many people on the boat. The deck was very quiet. I sat in one chair and put my feet on another chair. The sea was very blue and it was warm in the sun. I fell asleep.

When I woke up we were passing Serifos. It's the island before Sifnos. Serifos is like Sifnos; the houses are all white and square like pieces of sugar. It's very pretty. As the boat got close to the land I could smell the plants and see the purple of the mountains.

I was very happy. I love the Greek islands, but I didn't know Sifnos. There are so many islands in Greece, you can only know a few of them. I took my guidebook out of my bag and began to read. I knew some of the history of the island already. 'Lots of places to visit,' I thought. I turned the page.

Sifnos was once very rich, the guidebook told me, because of its gold and mines. I knew that. I've seen the Treasury of Sifnos in Delphi. Many, many years ago, the Greeks thought that Delphi was the centre of the world.

'Like Stavros,' I thought. 'He often says that Greece is the centre of the world.'

Many years ago the Greeks built a great temple to the sun god Apollo in Delphi. Every year everyone in Greece had to give something to Apollo's temple in Delphi. They gave Apollo the best fruit and gold from the gold mines.

They always gave Apollo the best. The Treasury was where the people of Sifnos kept the gold which they gave to the Temple of Apollo in Delphi. They built it two thousand five hundred years ago.

But there was a story in my guidebook that I didn't know. One year, the people of Sifnos said, 'Why do we do this? We need the gold, too.' And they made an egg and put gold only on the outside. 'Apollo will never know,' they said, and they went to Delphi with their egg which was only gold on the outside. But Apollo knew that the egg from Sifnos was not the same as a gold egg. He was very, very angry and he made the gold mines on Sifnos fall into the sea. And that is where they are today. And there is no more gold on Sifnos.

I liked the story. I didn't know if you could still see the old gold mines. 'I'll ask Eleni,' I thought.

Soon the boat arrived in Sifnos. In front of all the cars on the boat was a line of old ladies in black. They were all carrying big bags and stood waiting to get off. They looked like runners at the beginning of a marathon. Then the boat stopped and the old ladies ran forward. I laughed. It's always the same on Greek boats. The grandmothers are the first to get off.

I didn't run. I wasn't in a hurry. The boat arrived at the little harbour of Kamares. I could see cafés and *tavernas*. It was lunchtime and I was hungry.

'I'll have lunch here,' I thought, 'and then go to Poulati.'

I walked along the harbour. There were lots of fishing boats but also one very big motor yacht. There were three men on it.

'Hello, beautiful!' one of the men called. I hate it when

men call at me like that. I looked at him. He was dark with a black moustache. Beside him sat another man reading a newspaper. He didn't look at me.

'Hi!' the first man called again. 'Come and have lunch with us.'

There was a third man. He looked younger than the others. He looked about my age, twenty-seven. The other

men looked about ten years older. The younger man was tall and slim and good-looking. But he didn't smile at me.

'Go away,' he said. 'We're busy.'

'Don't listen to Takis,' said the first man. 'You can come here any time. We always like to see a pretty girl.'

'Shut up, Mike,' said the man called Takis. He turned away and went down the stairs inside the yacht.

I walked away. I didn't like them and I didn't want to go on their yacht. But the young man, Takis, made me angry. Why did he say 'Go away' to me like that? He didn't have to speak to me like that. I wasn't doing anything. But I soon forgot him because I loved Kamares.

There was just one road and lots of little *taverna*s beside the sea. I sat down and asked for a Greek salad and some fish. Near the *taverna* was a shop selling gold jewellery.

'More gold,' I thought. 'Why does everyone want it so much? Why is gold so special and not silver? What is it about gold?'

I sat in the little restaurant and looked at the sea. I ate some fish and thought about gold. 'Who were the very first people who used gold?' I asked myself. I knew that once, but I couldn't remember.

A man once wrote that people prefer gold to life. Of course it's not true. Everyone prefers life to anything else, but I understand what he meant. People will do anything for gold. Everyone wants gold. Many people have died for gold. Gold is dangerous.

Chapter 3 *Poulati*

I took a taxi to Poulati and I met Eleni and Yiannis. They were very friendly. Eleni showed me Stavros's house. I loved it. The house was just above the beach, and it had a small garden. It was very quiet. I sat down in the garden and looked at the sea. 'I will get well here quickly,' I thought. Stavros was right. This is a very special place.

What can I say about Poulati? It has a beach and a small harbour with a few fishing boats. There is Eleni's *taverna* and a shop that is also the village café and bar. But that does not tell you very much. You can say the same about most Greek fishing villages. But Poulati is different.

Is it that everything is white? The houses are white, the church is white, and even the paths between the houses are white.

Or perhaps what I love about Poulati is the feeling that everything has been there for ever. Of course that's not true. The plastic chairs in the café are new and some of the houses are new, but it feels old. The village feels as old as the mountain behind the village and the rocks under the sea.

Or maybe it's the colour of the sea. Blue as a winter sky without clouds but also green. The sea is green where it covers the large flat rocks on one side of the harbour and, further out, it is blue and green. And then just blue. Blue until it meets the sky.

Yes, that's why I love Poulati. Because of the sea. I sat in the garden that first afternoon and I saw only the sea and a few small boats. Nothing moved, but very slowly the colour of the sea changed. You can sit all day and just watch the sea. In the cafés, the old men sit every day and watch the sea.

Once, the old men were fishermen, but now they watch the young fishermen go out in their boats. And watch them come back with fresh fish for all the people of Poulati. And some for the main town of Apollonia, which is in the middle of Sifnos, on the other side of the mountain.

The one road from Poulati goes to Apollonia. I soon found that there were only a few roads on Sifnos and only a very few cars. There were three or four buses every day which went to and from Apollonia, and there were taxis, too. But there were lots and lots of paths. Some of the paths were very, very old. They were stone paths and, as an archaeologist, I found them very interesting.

I wanted to walk all over the island along these paths, but I was still too tired. So, like the old men, I sat in the café and in my garden and I looked at the sea. Before I went to Sifnos, I thought that I was going to do lots of work on the island. I took lots of books to Sifnos. But I didn't open them. I just looked at the sea and watched the fishermen.

And soon I began to feel better. I went for short walks around Poulati and Apollonia.

It was very quiet walking along these paths. There were birds but no cars and only a few people. But there were often people in the fields. They smiled and waved. Often they stopped me. 'Come here! Come here!' they said. And then they gave me tomatoes and oranges. Or they said 'Come and eat with us.' And then I sat down in their fields and ate lunch with them: bread, goat's cheese and small, sweet onions. And we drank wine made from their grapes, and water. Sifnos, unlike many Greek islands, has lots of water.

Days passed very quickly. I got stronger every day. I love

walking and this was an island big enough for good walks. I started to go swimming, too. And in the evening I went to Eleni's *taverna*.

Sometimes I ate alone and sometimes I ate with Eleni's brother, Yiannis. Yiannis was a fisherman. I thought that he was about fifty years old, but it wasn't easy to say. Years of sun and wind and sea water made him look older.

Yiannis told me where I could find the best paths and he told me the names of the plants and the trees.

Yiannis always sat down and talked to me after dinner. He was very interested in archaeology, he said, and he showed me a small pottery cup.

'I found this in my garden,' Yiannis said. 'How old is it, Professor?' He always called me professor. It was his little joke. He liked to make me laugh. I always laughed when he called me professor.

'I don't know,' I replied. 'It could be two thousand years old or it could be fifty years old. The pottery here hasn't changed very much. It's the same now as it always was. If you want me to tell you the date of this pot, I must take it to Athens, to the university.'

'It's not important,' said Yiannis. 'The date isn't important. It's beautiful and that's all that matters.'

I smiled. 'That's true,' I said.

'When I was a boy,' Yiannis told me, 'there were five hundred potters working in Sifnos. Now there are eleven. People find pots from Sifnos all over Europe, and today many of the pots in Athens are still made by people from Sifnos,' he said. 'If you go to Marousi, outside Athens, where all the potteries are, you will find lots of potters from Sifnos.'

18

But I was more interested in the old pots. I like thinking about the past. I prefer the past to the present. Now. What do we know about now, about the present? Nothing. There isn't the time to find out. But when you try to find out about the past, there is lots of time. But then, I'm an archaeologist, as you know. The past is my country.

'Where are the old potteries on Sifnos?' I asked Yiannis.

'I'll show you,' he said.

In Eleni's *taverna*, as in all Greek *taverna*s, there were paper tablecloths on the tables. Some of the tablecloths had pictures of boats on them and some had maps of Sifnos. At my table, the tablecloth had a map of Sifnos. Yiannis took a pen out of his pocket and drew on the map.

'There used to be potteries here and here,' he said, 'and here and here.'

'What about that mark there?' I asked.

'That's Aghios Sostis,' said Yiannis.

'Was there a pottery at Aghios Sostis?' I asked.

'No,' said Yiannis. 'That's where you can find the gold mines.'

'Gold? I thought that there wasn't any gold on Sifnos now,' I said.

'You can find gold,' smiled Yiannis. 'Not a lot of gold, but a few bits here and there. Not many people know where it is. But I do. I'll take you there one day. I often go fishing near Aghios Sostis. It's a good place to find fish. There are caves under the water. The fish like that. And sometimes you can find bits of gold, too.'

'Really. Are you the only person who knows where the gold is? You must be careful,' I told Yiannis.

I was joking. We laughed. 'The professor is worried that

someone will take my gold,' Yiannis said to Eleni. She laughed. We all laughed.

I went home and fell asleep. When I woke up it was dark. There was a very loud noise. Then another. I ran outside.

Eleni was running along the beach. There was a fire in the harbour. One of the fishing boats was on fire.

'Yiannis!' Eleni shouted. 'Yiannis!'

Chapter 4 *The fire*

I ran back into the house and put on my jeans and a pullover. Then I ran down to the beach. Lots of other people were running to the beach, too. Everyone was shouting.

It was Yiannis's boat on fire. I knew the boat. It was

painted white outside and green inside. It was a beautiful little boat and Yiannis loved it. But where was Yiannis?

I ran along the beach shouting, 'Yiannis!' I shouted again, 'Yiannis!'

I couldn't see him and he didn't answer. There was still a lot of smoke coming from the boat.

Then, suddenly, there was another very loud noise. And then it was very, very quiet. There was just the sound of the sea.

And now there was no boat on the sea, just a few bits of wood. No fire and no smoke.

Eleni fell down onto the sand crying. The other women in the village went to help her. I didn't know what to do. I saw Nikos, the policeman from Apollonia, and a group of fishermen. I walked up to them.

'What happened?' Nikos asked one of the fishermen.

'I don't know,' the fisherman answered. 'I woke up when I saw the fire. Yiannis was still inside the boat. I think he was asleep. But the fire was too quick. I couldn't help him.'

There was several empty wine bottles on the harbour wall. Nikos picked up a bottle.

'Perhaps Yiannis drank too much wine,' said Nikos. 'I think that's what happened. Yiannis drank too much wine and didn't know what he was doing. It's very sad,' Nikos said. 'I feel very sorry for his sister, Eleni.'

The fishermen looked at each other. After Nikos walked away, one of them said, 'I don't believe any of that. Yiannis didn't drink. And that boat was all that he had. It was his work and his life. You've seen him. He washed it every day. He loved that boat. I don't understand it.'

'I don't believe it, either,' said another fisherman. 'But what can we do? Yiannis is dead. We must help Eleni now.'

I didn't know Yiannis very well, but I liked him. Stavros knew Yiannis very well. 'I must tell Stavros,' I thought.

There wasn't a telephone in the house. 'I go to Poulati to get away from work,' Stavros told me. 'No newspapers and no telephone calls.' There was a telephone in Eleni's *taverna*, but I didn't want to go there. She needed to be with her friends. So I took the first bus to Apollonia to phone Stavros. He was in his office.

'Something terrible has happened,' I told him. I told him about the fire and about Yiannis and his boat.

'Oh no,' said Stavros. 'I've known Yiannis for years and years. I can't believe it. Not Yiannis. Poor Eleni.'

'Yes,' I agreed. 'It's terrible for Eleni.'

'What happened?' asked Stavros.

I told him what the fisherman told Nikos, and about the bottles of wine.

'I don't believe it,' said Stavros. 'Yiannis drank a glass of wine with his dinner. But he didn't drink bottles of wine. I've known Yiannis for twenty years. I can't believe it,' he said again.

'I'll come out,' he said. 'I'll get the next boat to Sifnos. I must come and see Eleni. Are you OK or do you want to come back to Athens?' he asked me.

'No,' I said. 'I'll stay here.'

'OK,' he said. But now he was crying. 'Yiannis! It's terrible. I can't believe it. What's my wife going to say? Yiannis is an old friend of ours. We've known him for so many years . . .'

I was crying, too. 'Last night we were laughing together

and now he's dead. We were laughing about someone killing him and now he's dead.'

'I don't understand,' said Stavros. 'No-one wanted Yiannis dead.'

'I don't mean that,' I said. 'He told me about fishing at Aghios Sostis and that there were still bits of gold in the sea there. We were laughing. It was nothing.'

'I see,' said Stavros. 'But there isn't any gold on Sifnos.'

'I know,' I said. 'We were just laughing together.'

'Oh,' said Stavros. There was nothing else to say. Yiannis was dead.

I took the bus back from Apollonia. I was very sad. I sat in the garden and tried to read a book. But I didn't feel like reading.

I think I fell asleep, because the next thing I heard was two men shouting. I was sitting behind a large tree, so they couldn't see me.

'I've done what you said,' shouted the first man. 'But a man's dead now.'

'It's not my fault,' said the second man. 'I didn't know they were going to kill anyone.'

'But why kill him?' shouted the first man. I thought that he sounded like Nikos, the policeman.

'They saw him fishing near Aghios Sostis,' said the second man. 'I thought that they were going to tell him not to go there. I didn't know that they were going to kill him.'

Chapter 5 *The man called Takis*

The men were still shouting. I stood up very quietly. I wanted to find out who they were. I was right. One of them was Nikos, the policeman. And I knew the other man, too. He was one of the men on the yacht that first morning. The man they called Takis, who told me to go away. I didn't like the good-looking man. What was he doing here? Why was he talking to Nikos?

I sat down again and waited until they left. I wanted to speak to Stavros again, but I didn't want to talk in the *taverna*. Someone could hear me. But there wasn't another bus that day. So I started to walk. It was an hour to Apollonia and I was very tired when I got there.

I phoned Stavros. He wasn't in his office, but I found him at home.

'Liz?' he asked. 'What is it? Are you OK?'

I told Stavros about Nikos and the man called Takis. 'Nikos said that someone killed Yiannis.'

'That's terrible,' said Stavros. 'But why?'

'Because Yiannis was fishing near Aghios Sostis. The man said that they didn't want him near Aghios Sostis. But I don't know who "they" are. Do you think that they've found gold, in the old mines?'

'Apollo's gold! That old story. No, I don't think so. Lots and lots of people have looked in those mines, Liz. There's no gold there now.'

'But why kill Yiannis? It's terrible. And I can't go to the police because Nikos is a policeman.'

'Did you say that the other man, Takis, was on a yacht?' asked Stavros.

'Yes,' I answered. 'The yacht was in Kamares when I arrived. It was the biggest motor yacht I've ever seen.'

'How many men were on the yacht?' Stavros asked.

'There were three on the deck. One of them spoke to me. They called him Mike. One of them was sitting down. He was wearing a lot of gold,' I said. 'And the third man was the one called Takis. He's the man I saw this afternoon with Nikos.'

'A big yacht and men wearing gold,' said Stavros. He was thinking. 'Did you see any diving things on the yacht?' he asked.

'No,' I said. 'But that doesn't mean there isn't any. It was a very big yacht.'

I knew what Stavros was thinking. Stealing. Diving into the sea and finding pots or other valuable things. And selling them. You can buy lots of gold jewellery if you sell even one small Greek pot.

'Do you think that the men on the yacht have found something in the sea near Aghios Sostis?' I asked Stavros. 'Perhaps they've found a statue.'

There's a famous Greek statue which was found in the sea not very far from Sifnos. It was found near Milos, which is the next island to Sifnos. You can see Milos from Sifnos. The statue is in the Louvre Museum in Paris. It's called the *Venus de Milo*.

'Perhaps they've found another *Venus de Milo*,' I said. 'What do you think?' I asked Stavros.

'I don't know,' said Stavros. 'But I'll talk to some people here. The police in Athens may know something about them. But these men are dangerous, Liz.'

'Yes,' I said.

'So don't do anything yourself,' said Stavros. 'Don't go near these men. Stay in Poulati.'

'Will you be here tomorrow?' I asked Stavros.

'No,' he said. 'There isn't a boat tomorrow. I'm coming on Tuesday. And don't go to Kamares without me. I know you, Liz. You always want to find out everything. You don't like waiting.'

'I won't do anything stupid,' I said.

'Good,' said Stavros. 'Because these men are dangerous. Remember that. They've already killed a man.'

'I'll remember,' I said.

But as I came out of the telephone office I saw Mike from the yacht. He was sitting in a café drinking coffee. He waved to me.

'Hello, beautiful,' he said. 'Are you coming to see us?'

'I don't know,' I said. 'Maybe.'

'Come and have lunch with us tomorrow,' he said. 'We'll go out in the yacht. I'll show you the island.'

'Perhaps they have found a pot or statue or something under the sea,' I thought. 'It's only lunch. I'll just have a look round the yacht. And then I can tell Stavros when he comes.'

'That sounds very nice,' I said. 'But I can't stay long.'

'That's OK,' he said. He was smiling.

*   *   *

The next day I took the bus to Kamares and walked along

the road to the yacht. As I stepped onto the boat, Takis
came up the stairs from inside.

'What are you doing here?' he asked. 'Go away. We don't
want you here.' He was angry.

But Mike was behind him.

'I asked her to come on the yacht for lunch, Takis,' he
said. 'Is there a problem?'

'Yes,' said Takis. 'We don't want her here and we don't
have time to stop for lunch, Mike.'

'Don't listen to Takis,' said Mike. 'He works too hard.'
Mike put his arm around my shoulders. 'We're going to
have fun, you and I. I know it.'

Chapter 6   *On the yacht*

The yacht was very big. It wasn't a pretty yacht. It was just big and fast. I hated it. I like yachts that look like the Greek fishing boats.

At first I only saw the main room downstairs. Mike said that there were some very nice bedrooms, but I didn't want to see them. Not with Mike. Apart from Mike and Takis, there was the boss.

The boss was called Mr John. He was also the captain of the yacht. Mr John didn't say very much. So I didn't know where he came from. And he looked at me as if I wasn't there. I didn't like him. In fact, I didn't like any of them.

We left Kamares and sailed north. I lay in the sun and closed my eyes. 'Perhaps they'll think that I'm asleep,' I thought. 'Then I can listen to what they are saying.'

The first voice I heard was Takis. 'We'll be close to a beach soon, Mike,' he said. 'Why don't you get off there with the woman? You can have some fun. We can come back for you later.'

'You never stop, Takis, do you?' answered Mike. 'What's your problem? Don't you like women?'

'I like women,' said Takis. 'But not when I'm working. What happens if she sees . . . ?'

I couldn't hear the next bit. They were speaking very quietly. 'She won't see anything,' said Mike. 'She's just a stupid tourist.'

'How do you know she's stupid?' asked Takis.

'Well,' said Mike. 'She's pretty. And pretty girls are all stupid.'

'Pretty girls are stupid,' I thought. 'So that's what you think. How wrong you are. But if you want to think that I'm stupid, that's fine.'

We had lunch. The yacht was going round the island. We passed a village and a beach. There were people swimming. Then there was nothing and no-one. Just grey rock. It was very, very quiet. Mr John was talking to someone but I couldn't hear what they were saying. The yacht was closer to the land now, very close. There were no beaches here. It wasn't like Poulati. The yacht stopped.

I looked up and all I could see was rock. About twenty metres high, I thought. And it wasn't the kind of rock that you could climb. It was straight, like the wall of a house.

I was beginning to feel very afraid. I was alone on a boat and there was nothing but sea and rock. If I shouted, no-one could hear me. Why didn't I listen to Stavros?

Mike came up. 'Would you like to go downstairs for a rest, Liz?' he asked me. 'I'm sure that you're tired.'

'I'm OK here,' I said.

'That's not very friendly,' said Mike. 'And I thought that you were my friend.'

'Can't we just sit and talk here?' I asked him.

'What do you want to talk about?' he asked me.

'Oh, I don't know,' I said. I smiled and tried to sound stupid. 'You must be very clever to have a big yacht like this. What do you do?' I asked him.

He smiled and put his hand on my knee. 'This and that.

We buy and sell. Nothing to worry your pretty little head about.'

I smiled at him. 'Buy and sell,' I thought. 'Buy and sell what?'

'You make it sound very easy,' I said. 'But I'm sure I couldn't do it.'

'A pretty girl like you doesn't have to work,' said Mike. 'I could look after you. If you were nice to me.'

'Nice to you,' I thought. 'I can't think of anything worse.'

'Come here,' said Mike. 'Give me a kiss.'

'No! Please,' I said. 'No. I'm not like that.'

'Then what are you doing here?' asked Mike.

I jumped up. 'Go away,' I said. 'Go away and leave me alone.'

'Go away where?' Mike laughed. 'There's only the yacht. And you and me.'

He put his arm around my shoulders. I pulled his arm away and ran downstairs.

'Help me!' I shouted. 'Somebody help me!' But I knew that there was no-one on the yacht who could help me.

I ran through the main room and opened the first door I saw. It was a bedroom. And there was a lock on the door. I ran inside and locked the door. Mike was following me. I opened another door. I didn't know what I was doing. It was a cupboard and it was full of guns.

'Oh, no,' I said when I saw the guns. 'Oh, no. Who are these people?'

At that moment Mike came in. He was smiling.

'There is more than one key to every lock,' he said. Then he saw the open cupboard.

'Oh dear,' he said. 'That was very stupid. Why did you

open that cupboard? Now we will have to kill you.' He pulled out a gun.

'Hey Mike!' It was Takis. 'Wait!'

'Now what's your problem?' asked Mike.

'I don't have a problem,' said Takis. 'But Mr John wants you in his office. And why hurry? Why kill her now? Why don't I tie her up and then we can have some fun with her? You can kill her later.'

Mike smiled. 'I like that,' he said. 'Tie her up.'

Takis came towards me. In his hand was a gun.

Chapter 7   *Terrorists*

Takis took me up out of the room and up the stairs. We were outside. He put his gun into his pocket.

'Be very quiet,' he said. 'We only have a few moments before Mike finds out that Mr John doesn't want to see him. Then Mike will come back and Mike, as you know, is not a nice man.'

'I don't understand,' I said. 'I thought you were going to kill me.'

'No,' said Takis. 'I'm trying to help you. Can you swim underwater?' he asked.

'Yes,' I replied. 'But aren't you one of them?'

'No, I'm not one of them,' said Takis. 'I work for an international police force. But they think I'm one of them.'

'Interpol?' I asked. I began to understand. 'We work with Interpol at the university.'

'Why didn't you listen to me?' Takis asked. 'I told you not to come.'

'I thought I could find out what they were doing,' I said. 'What have they found?' I asked. 'Is it a statue? An old pot?'

'A statue? A pot? What are you talking about?' Takis asked me. 'Are you mad? These men are terrorists. They're here to sell guns.'

'Guns,' I said. I felt ill. 'I thought that they were stealing old pots,' I said. 'I'm an archaeologist.'

'I see,' said Takis. He smiled. He had a nice smile. 'And that's why you wanted to find out what they were doing?'

There was a noise from below.

'Quick,' said Takis. 'That must be Mike. Jump into the sea. You can swim under the rock there.' He pointed. 'On the other side is the beach of Aghios Sostis. There's a cave there. And that's where the mines begin. Go into the mines and stay there until I come and get you. I have to stay here. There are some men coming tonight to buy the guns. I have to know who they are.'

At that moment Mike came back onto the deck. He looked very angry.

'Go! Now!' said Takis.

'What's going on, Takis?' shouted Mike.

I jumped into the sea.

'Stop!' shouted Mike. He took out his gun.

I swam under the water and felt something go past me. Mike was shooting at me, but nothing hit me. I was OK. I swam to the back of the boat and put my head above the water. Mike was shouting at Takis but I couldn't see them.

'Why did you let her go?' Mike was shouting.

'She was a pretty girl, why not?' answered Takis.

Then I heard a heavy noise. I swam forward a bit. I saw Mike hit Takis. Takis fell down.

'What's happening?' said another voice. It was Mr John.

'I don't know, Mr John,' said Mike. 'I think we have a problem. Takis didn't kill the girl. She's seen the guns and she's gone.'

'And why did he do that?' asked Mr John.

'I don't know, boss,' said Mike. 'Takis didn't tell me.'

'Is he dead?' asked Mr John.

'No,' I thought. 'Not dead, please.'

'No,' said Mike. 'I just hit him. He hit his head on the side of the boat. He'll wake up later.'

'When he wakes up I want to talk to him,' said Mr John. 'I have a lot of questions for Takis. He worries me. In this job you can't have men who worry you. What about the woman? You were stupid, Mike, to bring her.'

'Sorry, boss,' said Mike. 'You know me and women.'

'Yes, I do,' said Mr John. 'One day you will die because of a woman. Now, what about this one?'

'I think she was just afraid. She was just a stupid English tourist. Anyhow, I shot her as she jumped into the sea. I think that she's dead. She hasn't come up.'

I wasn't dead, but I was very afraid.

'I want you to watch for the woman,' said Mr John. 'If she's alive, you'll soon see her. There's only rock here. There's nowhere for her to go. If you don't see her, then we know she's dead.'

'Yes, boss,' said Mike.

'Now, tie Takis up.' Mr John was very angry. 'I'm going to phone a friend of mine. Takis says that he knows him very well. I believed him. Now I'm not so sure. Tell me when Takis wakes up. I want to talk to him. First, he can tell me why he let the woman go. Then he can tell me who he is. And then I will kill him.'

'Oh no,' I thought. 'This is terrible. And it's my fault. Why did I ever get on the yacht? They are going to kill Takis because he helped me. Now I have to help Takis. But how?'

Chapter 8   *In the cave*

I'm not Superman. I'm not even Superwoman. But I did swim under the rocks to the beach on the other side. When you are afraid, you can do things that you can't usually do.

After that I was very, very tired, so I sat on the beach and looked at the sea. It was late afternoon and there was no wind. The sea was like glass. When the sea is quiet like that, the Greeks say that the sea is like oil. Sometimes when I fly to Greece, I look down and there is the sea below, like glass, like oil. It is the colour of gold and the islands are blue. There is nothing more beautiful than looking down on to the Greek islands from the air. That is the gold that I love. That is the real gold of the Greek islands. The sun on the sea.

I sat on the beach for a while and then I stood up. The cave was on one side of the beach and it was big enough to walk into.

'What do I do now?' I thought. 'I can't stay here. Takis isn't going to come and help me. The men are going to kill him. They are going to kill him because he saved my life. I must do something.'

The cave was full of big boxes. One of the boxes was half open. I looked inside. It was full of guns, machine guns.

At that moment I wanted to be Superwoman. I wanted to say: 'Ah! a machine gun, just what I want.' Superwoman could make a boat from the side of one of the boxes, and

jump onto the yacht. She could take a gun and kill all the bad men and save Takis. But I wasn't Superwoman. I didn't know how to use a gun. I didn't know what to do.

I walked round the cave looking for something, but I

didn't know what I was looking for. I wanted to save Takis, but I didn't know what to do.

'I need to find the mines,' I thought. The back of the cave was dark. I put my hand in my pocket to get my torch, so I could see. There are always three things in my pockets. One is a torch to help me see in the dark, one is a magnifying glass and one is my Swiss army knife. All archaeologists use knives. We use them for cutting. We use them when we find things in the ground.

'If I could get back to the yacht,' I thought, 'I could cut Takis free.'

I walked down the beach. I couldn't swim back under the rock. I was too tired to swim underwater again. But I could swim slowly round the rock, back to the yacht. It was getting dark now. No-one was going to see me. I walked into the sea and began to swim. Then I heard it. It was the sound of the yacht. It was getting louder. Then I saw the yacht coming round the rocks and straight towards me.

I began to swim back to the beach but someone saw me. I heard Mike's voice: 'It's her. It's the woman. Liz!'

Chapter 9 *Caught*

'Don't shoot her, Mike.' It was Mr John. 'I want to talk to her first. Hey!' he shouted at me. 'You there! Stand up! Put your hands on your head!'

I was almost back on the beach now. I stood up. Mr John had a gun too. I put my hands on my head.

'What are you doing here?' he asked. 'How did you get here? No-one saw you swim round the rock.'

'Well, I did,' I said. 'I swam round the rock. How else could I get here?'

I wasn't going to tell him that Takis knew you could swim under the rock.

'I ask the questions,' said Mr John. 'But you weren't swimming towards the beach just now,' he said. 'You were swimming away from it.'

'I wanted to get away,' I replied. 'I didn't know where I was going. I was afraid.'

'I don't believe you,' said Mr John. 'And I don't think you're as stupid as Mike thinks you are. But I haven't got time for you now.' Mr John turned to Mike. 'Mike,' he said, 'tie up the woman and put Takis in the cave with her. We'll come and get them tomorrow morning. We have to meet our friends tonight. I don't want these two on the yacht when our friends arrive.'

Mike came and tied me up. I could see that he enjoyed doing it. He pushed me down onto the beach. I hit my head. It hurt.

Then someone carried Takis off the yacht onto the beach. Mike picked him up and pushed him down beside me. Then they took most of the boxes and put them onto the yacht. And the yacht left.

I didn't know if Takis was dead or alive. It was getting darker now, but there was still just enough light to be able to see.

'Takis,' I said, quietly. 'Takis!' Takis opened his eyes. He looked terrible. There was blood on his face.

'Liz,' he said. But it was difficult for him to speak. His teeth were broken. And there was blood on his lips.

'Why didn't you go into the mine?' said Takis.

'I wanted to help you,' I said. 'I had a knife. I thought I could cut you free.'

'Have you still got the knife?' he asked.

'Yes,' I said. 'Mike didn't look in my pockets. But I can't get it. My hands are tied behind my back.'

'Maybe I can get to it,' Takis said. He slowly sat up. I could see that it was difficult and that it hurt him.

'Are you OK?' I asked him.

'I don't know,' he said. 'My head hurts and my leg hurts. I think it's broken. But I'll do what I can.'

I moved round so that his hands were beside my pocket. It wasn't easy for him to get the knife out of my pocket, but he did it. He opened the knife and cut himself free. And then he cut my hands free, too.

'Now what do we do?' I asked him. 'We can't sit and wait for them to come back. We have to get out of here.'

Takis tried to stand up but then fell down again.

'I can't stand,' he said. 'I'll have to stay here. Get me a

gun from that open box and then go. Run into the mines. Don't let them find you!'

I went to the box and pulled out two guns. I gave one to Takis, but he couldn't take it. There was blood on his shoulder.

'I'm not leaving you,' I told him.

'Then they'll kill both of us.'

'Show me how to use the gun,' I said. Takis showed me what to do.

'They aren't Greek are they, these men?' I asked Takis.

'No,' said Takis. 'They come from different countries.'

'But why are they here in Greece?'

'That's a good question,' said Takis. 'You see,' he began, 'Greece is the centre of the world . . .'

I smiled.

'Why are you smiling?' he asked me.

'It's just that a friend of mine often says that.' I thought of Stavros. I was never going to see Stavros again . . .

'It's true,' said Takis. He drew a map in the sand with his finger. 'Greece is here, in the centre. You have Russia and the Balkans here, and Africa here, and the Middle East is here,' he said. 'Greece is in the middle. And all the terrorists come here. And we don't want them. It makes us very angry. We don't want these people in our country. My job is to stop them.'

We talked a little. It wasn't easy for Takis to talk because he was badly hurt. He needed to go to a hospital, but there was nothing I could do.

'Do you have a wife?' I asked Takis. 'Children?'

'No,' Takis said. 'Only my mother and father. I don't think I could do this job if there were children in my life.'

'Are you married?' he asked me.

'I was married,' I told him.

So, we talked. Takis spoke very good English. He was also interested in archaeology and books and music. We were interested in lots of the same things. He told me about his own home which was in the north of Greece. I told him about my job and he told me about his.

'I studied English at university,' he said. 'But I didn't want to be a teacher.' Then we started to talk about Greece.

After a while we stopped talking. Then Takis began to sing a song very quietly. It was an old song, a very unhappy song about dying. Greeks always sing. They sing when they are sad and when they are happy.

After an hour or two, I heard the yacht again.

'They're coming back,' Takis said. He lay back on the ground, his hands behind his back.

The first one to come into the cave was Mike. He was smiling. I think he had the worst smile I have ever seen. He turned his gun towards Takis.

'Mr John has decided that he doesn't need to talk to you. So, it's goodbye.'

Chapter 10   *Apollo's Gold*

I don't know how I did it or what I actually did. But I lifted the gun. The noise was terrible, but Mike was dead.

'Be careful with that gun,' shouted Takis. 'You nearly killed me, too.'

I put down the gun.

'Liz.' Takis spoke more quietly. 'It's OK. It's OK. Don't worry. You did what you had to do. I'm sorry I shouted at you. But now just do what I say and get back into the mine. Mr John will be here any moment. I don't want anything to happen to you.'

'I'm not leaving you alone like this,' I said.

I went to pick up the gun.

'Don't move,' said a voice. It was Mr John. 'Get back,' he said to me. I moved back away from the gun.

'You are beginning to make me angry,' said Mr John. 'That is not a good thing. And so I am going to kill you.'

He pointed the gun at me. I could see Takis trying to get up, but he wasn't strong enough.

Then I heard something else outside. It was another boat. It was coming towards the beach. Mr John turned round.

'This is the police,' someone shouted. 'Put down your guns.' Then Mr John put his arm around my neck.

'If you come any closer, this woman dies,' he shouted. But at that moment there was the noise of a gun, and Mr John fell backwards. Then a large man ran into the cave. A

man I knew very well. Stavros! Nikos the policeman was
with him. He was holding a gun.

'Is everyone OK?' said Stavros.

'Yes,' I said. 'I think so. How did you find us?'

'Nikos was working with Takis to catch the terrorists,'
said Stavros. 'When I couldn't find you in Poulati I spoke
to the police, to Nikos. He saw you get on the yacht. And
Takis had told us the yacht was coming here.'

I started to laugh. And then I started to cry.

*   *   *

The police took Takis and me to a hospital in Athens. They sent me home after one day, but Takis stayed in hospital for a week. I visited him nearly every day.

I also met with Stavros every day. We both felt very sad about Yiannis. In the summer holidays, seven weeks after Yiannis had died, Stavros and his family went back to Poulati to be with Eleni.

I stayed in Athens and, one afternoon in June, while I was at home reading, my doorbell rang. It was Takis. I was really pleased to see him. We talked for a bit. He told me that Mr John and some other men were now in prison.

'Nikos and the police found the men who bought the guns,' Takis said.

'And I've got something for you, Liz.' He gave me a small brown stone. 'You told me how much you liked the story of Apollo's gold,' he said, 'so this is for you. I found it in the mines. It's gold.'

'Thank you,' I told him. 'Thank you very much.' I took his hand. 'But I think I found something better than gold in Aghios Sostis.'

Takis smiled at me. 'I'm glad you feel like that, Liz,' he said. 'Because I feel like that, too . . .'